POETRY
now

LOVE EVERLASTING

Edited by

Joanne Baxter

First published in Great Britain in 2000 by
POETRY NOW
Remus House,
Coltsfoot Drive,
Woodston,
Peterborough, PE2 9JX
Telephone (01733) 898101
Fax (01733) 313524

HB ISBN 0 75430 813 8
SB ISBN 0 75430 814 6

FOREWORD

Although we are a nation of poets we are accused of not reading poetry, or buying poetry books. After many years of listening to the incessant gripes of poetry publishers, I can only assume that the books they publish, in general, are books that most people do not want to read.

Poetry should not be obscure, introverted, and as cryptic as a crossword puzzle: it is the poet's duty to reach out and embrace the world.

The world owes the poet nothing and we should not be expected to dig and delve into a rambling discourse searching for some inner meaning.

The reason we write poetry (and almost all of us do) is because we want to communicate: an ideal; an idea; or a specific feeling. Poetry is as essential in communication, as a letter; a radio; a telephone, and the main criteria for selecting the poems in this anthology is very simple: they communicate.

CONTENTS

Love Poem (Rough Draft)

Stereotypical,
that burns a constant,
that views passion as past and adoration as now,
that worships good and expels impurity;
a closed eye against a world of realities,
a silent kingdom of total devotion.

A million documented hearts, all as one,
gently awaiting any return in reliance upon faith,
faith that binds in mirrored knots,
trust that shields harming words;
so much complete in stillness of one self, to be,
for purpose and in knowledge,
thus lies love, entwined with its own predisposition.

Reality,
bringing harsh words of tempted anger,
sudden need and so little fulfilment,
no tradition to be broken as the world rages
then falls to the silence of one moment's worship.

A body that harbours little personality,
running from the chase and pursuing those in flight,
logic no part of the heat and ice that kiss -
kissing in so much the real world, all can see,
though maybe few.
All blinded.

Hoping and waiting to feel a single touch,
overwhelmed by expectation and rejection
not a part of stories and stereotypes,
calmed never so long as the love lives in a stormy night,
night after night and unsleeping,
and unpredictable.

Hannah Thomas

DEPARTURE TO DREAMLAND

Stars shine down above our heads
Sun sinks down to embrace the sea
Wind moves but remains unseen
As we depart for the twilight zone inside my head
Children inquire if it's time for bed
While shadows dance and create enchanting spells
Close your eyes: Set the sails as we depart off into enchanting seas
For God's Universe is both untamed and vast
Filled with wonders that our forefathers once spoke of
Where mothers hold their young at night
Dismissing phantoms and the dark
Protective arms hold and shield
As lullabies float by on an unseen breeze
A land where treasures lie on virgin soil
Nightmares wage wars deep inside my mind's
Angry - psychological combat zones
Hauling the spirit both to and fore this was my life long ago
But I'm free at last to come and go as I please
To walk in happiness with my one true love
So cool dark night that awaits the dawn
Thank you for taking me to this pleasure dome inside my head.

Kathryn Morgan-Jones

LIES AND CYANIDE

Sitting there by the fireside,
with naked thoughts of cyanide,
when the one you've trusted has lied,
and loneliness is the one by your side,
and the only place you want to be . . . is in love.
Here you sit with a memory full of names,
different rules but the same old games,
wasted chances and bogus phone calls,
a depressing prison with lonelier walls,
and with no one at your side,
and in love you want to hide.
Oh the beer and the pills please stay away,
even though you can't face another day,
the joy of love is warped with dismay,
and the memories rich but too few,
yes there has been too many I love you's
and kiss to many always,
and still you face lonely days,
and love won't come knocking at your door,
because it don't come here no more,
so tell me, what are you crying for?
Freedom you can taste the morning sun,
life so rich for you it's just begun,
because now you can do what is best,
and plenty of time for the rest,
yet when there is no feeling inside,
because in love you want to hide,
when burning pictures is your pastime
and the what ifs plague your mind,
but how you please, all you want to be . . . is in love.

D Hobson

An Open Heart

I sit pen poised but for once my words lay dormant, yet
my thoughts shine so luminous in the caverns of my mind.
You are a woman now but to me that small girl still exists.
Through you I have tasted every one of life's dwelling emotions,
and in return I have found more treasures than this world could ever
afford. Oh the sweet charge of early innocence, those heart-rending
tears of hurt and pain and the bitter sweet thrill of adolescent love, the
frustrations and excitements of an ever changing world and
the sharp realities of a demanding world. But on that ocean of life
though tossed and turned with every wave, a deep and lasting bond
still remains. The pride I feel of the affection instilled in all those
around you fills me with gratitude that they too share my thoughts
of you. One day dear daughter I shall leave you, though you will
face pain and sorrow, remember; I will leave in your heart that which
will live forever, *My love.*

Terry White

Our Paul

I study your face on the photograph
Recalling the ways in which you made us laugh
Your sense of humour was next to none
You filled our lives with joy and fun
Today your smile lives on
All I can wait for is a bright new dawn
Today my tears still fall
They always will for my son, Paul.

Should I live a hundred years
My heart will ache, my eyes shed tears
For the special boy to whom I gave life
For whom I dreamt of finding a wife
To see him grown up with family too
Dreams and hopes which Death slew
In two more days an inquest will hear
Of the tragic accident which cost us so dear.

If love could have saved you Son
You would still be here.

Sorrowmum

Goddesses Of The Hearth

In my first house
she was my Margareta
who captivated me. Blonde hair
cut pudding-basin short,
a figure which one day
would stretch to maternity
but now was pleasure itself,
and cheeks like pink marshmallow.
For all time
she was my inspiration and my dream.

Then we moved again,
and lovely petal powdered
her face till it dimply sparkled like castor
on a soft sponge cake.
Her grey-green eyes deep-set, the hollows
drawn in by green, black shadow.
My dear one now was slim
so the veins stood out
like streams upon a map.
Almost cadaverous,
thin and fragile, yet lined like tissue,
for all time
she was my inspiration and my dream.

Yet now we move again they haunt me still.
Love was so often offered from apart,
so often rejected by understanding,
committed in another world -
as if they knew that would never satisfy
or elevate beyond the troubled
earth, save that by being
for all time my inspiration and my dream.

Eric Smith

ODE TO A FAITHFUL FRIEND

Jason is it 16 years
since you were a bundle of fluff
you were so small, and loved by all
you could have blown away with a puff.

Those days in the sun, when we were all young
wasn't it yesterday?
A beautiful collie, you grew so fast
a loving friend all the way.

We'd romp in the park, you'd run and you'd bark
so eager to make it all fun
your shiny black coat, that the judges would note
and the number of ribbons you won.

You had your own chair in our bedroom upstairs
and you'd curl up at night by the door
as time went by and the chair seemed too high
you slept by my bed on the floor.

That dreadful time when I came down to find
you sprawled in a heap by the stairs
the vet was so kind, she said you'd be fine
but you must never again climb up there.

Don't reproach me with your soulful eyes
when I go up to bed or a bath
it's only because I love you so much
that I now have to block your path.

Your tired old eyes find it hard to see now
and your bouncy legs have grown slow
you sleep a lot - do you dream a lot
of those sunny days long ago?

Dill Stimpson

UNCONDITIONALLY

I need not oath or statement,
To keep my love for you.
Come share my bed of heather
And drink the morning dew.
Clothe me in nature's raiments,
See me in pure moonlight,
Your nakedness would soothe me,
From demons of the night.

I need not gifts of untold wealth,
All I require from you
The last *peace* rose of summer,
Tied bow of midnight blue.
To know my favourite music,
To walk with flesh that's bare.
A kiss to banish fear away,
Till laughter rends the air.

I need not confirmation,
Tomorrow you'll be here,
For swiftly as a shooting star,
Love tends to disappear.
The rose you brought is fading,
The music's ending too,
But lasting, unconditional love,
Would be my gift to you.

J A Woodward

A Trail In Life

Who do you blame if a loved one is suddenly taken away?
More precious than gold, I thought was here to stay.

Where now for guidance or advice I could trust?
Where now for a shoulder to cry on or helping hands a must?

I know I'll never match your generosity in a thousand years,
I do try; your touch is always in my writing, this one in tears.

Looking forward to retirement, even now I wish it had been me,
Every day I prayed let me carry the illness God and set him free.

Reminders of you will come and go,
Some with a smile and others will roll a tear,
Sadness and emptiness will be lost in time,
However, memories will never disappear.

Displaying your example in life will be difficult you can see,
I never told you the strength of my faith; you are walking with me.

Nik Sharma

WHO ARE YOU?

You are everything to me
I share my life with you
You are my partner - my love
Advisor and Tutor
I cherish my being with you
You have been my instigator
To my life itself
But above all
You are my husband.

J Campbell Jones

Marnie-Lee

The day had come,
The time was right,
A healthy little baby girl,
Was born into our lives.
Her parents named her Marnie-Lee,
And Auntie Katie I'm so proud to be.
Weighing in at 7 pounds,
You lay there contentedly without a sound.
I saw you minutes after you were born,
All snuggled up safe and warm,
I sat and stared at your cot side,
Overwhelming happiness I couldn't control and hide.
Two little eyes so blue and bright,
Two tiny fists clasping so tight,
Little limbs so firm and fine,
Marnie-Lee the first niece of mine.
You have an angelic smile so sweet to see,
A priceless memory that will stay forever with me,
In your short time already, you've brought me so much pleasure,
Of which I can say could never be measured.
Already you're growing up really fast,
Your baby ways are a thing of the past,
You're learning new things every day,
From books, TV and the games we play.
I'll watch you grow and learn to walk,
And listen as you try to talk,
I'll help you learn your A,B,C's,
And help you count your 1,2,3's.
And when you venture into things exciting and new,
Remember Marnie-Lee my precious niece, Auntie Katie will always love you.

Katie Stratton

My Angel

*(Dedicated to my husband Daniel Keith
whom I met at The Angel Hotel, Abergavenny
on 16th June 1994, and married the same year
on Christmas Eve)*

Life would be so dull
without you in my life,
and I want you to know
my Angel
that I'm proud to be
your wife . . .
You are always there
for me,
through rain and shine,
through all the ups
and downs of life,
I'm so glad that you
are mine . . .
I wanted to tell you:
I love you,
But I guess you already
know,
I might not always say
it, and it might not
always show . . .
but there's not a day
that passes,
that I do not love you
true,

But for now, you can read
my thoughts,
and you will know that
I love you,
and I love you for being
My Angel
and I love you for being
You . . .

Jade Watkins

Heartbeat Of Love

Did your heart miss a beat today?
That's when love came your way
Did you feel your legs go weak?
That's when you both started to speak
Now you walk along together
Now you hope it will be forever
Then you look into each other's eyes
Now you know there will be no goodbyes.
So now your hearts beat as one
Now you know your love really has begun.

Sheryl Saxby

For The Love Of Louise

Slender beauty in front of me
Your presence drowns me like the sea.
Sweep me in and never fail
If you don't
I'll be beached like a whale!
With your passionate looks
I see you wherever I go
Whatever I do,
From Southampton to Heathrow.

You're a young beauty
With your life ahead,
I want to be a part of it
Before I'm dead.
The tide of life can be cruel
But it doesn't have to be the rule.
I am here for you
But I fear you don't know.
How far do I have to go?

Tim Saunders

Love

Speak softly to me
of your love.
Breathe my name
as you caress me.

Take my hand
and hold it gently.
To your heart
Which beats so strong.

Let the whisper
of your lips,
touch my face
So slowly, slowly.

Time and space
are all suspended,
in this hour
that's ours alone.

Youth is gone
and passion with it
but love is strong
and has no limit.

Joan Wills

BIG ISSUE

The carpet on the stair
Ends with the second flight.
There is no welcome there
And precious little light.
Yet up the scrubbed linoleum
I hear your halting footsteps come.

Listening with dismay
To those despondent feet
I am aware that they
Signal some new defeat.
Now your dejection has infected me
My love is nurse to your anxiety.

Eager I often wait
To hear you shout my name
With love articulate
And eyes aflame,
Indifferent to poverty and stress;
But you engulf me in your helplessness.

In comfortable age
Carpets will lap my door
For then I shall engage
Rooms on some lower floor.
But if I hear a lagging step above
I shall remember how it was to love.

Joan Gordon

TRIUNE - TO MY GIRL . . .

The grass it whispered to you among the breeze
Balming the scented smile of a summer rose
Beckoning, harmonising with nature's prose,
Inspired songs of shaded poems from unfelled trees.
Mountains flank the rocks, these are My Written Words.
Diamonds dust My Heartbeat in the sea for you.
Transforming tears, now pearls in the dew for you.
Mountains flank my love song written on the rocks.
Graceflakes calmed the storm of shadows now long gone.
No need to search your unborn's found his lady.
No need to search as rainbows star your baby.
My Grace it calmed the shadowed storms now long gone.
You recognised My Heartbeat now Three in One.
My girl the day's not ended, it's just begun.

A Tonner

Memories Galore

The earth stood still when we met once more,
weeping as we clasped each other tight,
it was a long, long time,
since I left for a distant shore.

So many memories and some regrets,
of places we went to, the things we did share,
not knowing where our destinies lay,
whatever the outcome we did not care.

A great deal of water has gone under the bridge,
times are now different for we have changed,
the love that we shared, it's not there anymore,
all we have left are memories galore.

Robert Gerald

BONNIE

You came when I was at my lowest
Just a small wee bundle of fur
With big brown eyes that mirrored my gaze
And I loved you.
Your look and your loving ways
You helped me over the one I'd lost
My broken heart began to heal
A bond grew.
So small I hold you in my arms
Your lick on my hand tells me all
Your nature so loving, your spirit so free
I love you dearly.
You have so much love to give
You're my happiness, so sweet your nature
What love could I need
That could be greater, than your love for me
The gift of love given so freely
No questions asked
From such a small being
We could learn that love is priceless
When given like yours.
You make my life worthwhile
You'll always be my own loving
Bonnie.

Hazel Webb

LETTER TO A FRIEND IN NORFOLK

Let us talk of Broadland, I don't want to hear the News.
Is a Barrage o'er the Yare something you would choose?
Should the volunteer fen-workers go on with 'Habitat Heaps'
Or should the clearing of a bank be something done for keeps?
Can you devise a way of controlling speeding boats . . .
Should it be on land, or better if it floats?
Well, a Mine was not precisely what I had in mind,
But now you come to mention it, it's tougher than a fine!
Have you noticed how the sunlight lies flecked in Salhouse Broad,
And shadow chases shadow down the river, never bored?
Or have you seen at Dilham on a roaring sunny day,
How there's still an air of peace, as if angels came to play
On the lazy spread of turf beside the sleepy little dyke,
And moorhens hide their children, almost anywhere they like.
If you've ever been to Geldeston, you'll know that near the lock
Are languid lengths of meadow, for a herd or for a flock,
And despite a thumping radio, shaking reed and sedge,
You can slip away to Yesterday, along the river's edge.
Ah yes, the Waveney, a lady gently born,
Drifting down to Beccles through a sunrise secret dawn -
And you can travel with her, keep your diesel slow,
And surprisingly enough the creatures seem to know
You're not a frightful monster, come to do them harm,
But go about their business without too much alarm.
Have you been through Martham Broad, and felt it was a place
That isn't quite within this world, something far and chaste?
But oh tell me, have you felt the weight of what we've
done to things?
I felt it on the Yare, a pain like leaden wings
That strove to rise above us, falling downward in defeat -
The only one resents us - Yare, sensing Man's deceit.

S Thomson

Love - Who You See

God is love,
Complete -
Without fear,
Fearless,
Pure, undiluted.

You first loved me.

I love God,
Constitutes
A lie,
My brother
I've seen.
This is the command,
'Love - who you see'

Ken Price

Love For Everyone

Every time I see you, every time you're near,
Every time I hear your voice, a lovely voice to hear;
Every time I look at you, every time you smile,
Suddenly my world turns around, and stays like that a while.
You have such a big effect on me;
You're unaware you do
I like to imagine, you love me, like I love you;
But of course I realise, it's just a game I play,
Because it's your vocation to love people every day.
So every time you smile like that,
It's for everyone, not just me,
Every time you look that way
Every time you speak,
Everyone will love you too,
Everyone you meet.

Barbara Stevens

ENIGMATIC COMPANION

Love drying rivers of tears born of disappointed frustration,
Partner through trials and tribulations you appear when needed most,
I waited with baited breath submerged in waves of anticipation,
Appearing again from those mists of time enigmatic comforting ghost.

Love what mysteries you unfold like births of each new spring,
Nightingales left far behind when they try to match your song,
Tossed and torn are my lonely senses new feelings you do bring,
Rainbows in mottled watery skies pale and fade in comparison.

Love heals wounded spirits, stir feelings that lie deep down,
Like morning mists lifting once more revealing filigree ferns of dew,
Crescendos of sweet music cross the mind in waves of rhythmic sound,
Forming bowers of primrose and bluebell blooming yellow and blue.

Love gently holding my trembling hand with your touch of tenderness,
Caught in gossamer webs of wonder captivated by inner feeling,
Swirling warm oceans of exhilaration born of your sweet caress,
Silver sand spread on shimmering beaches that sets my spirits reeling.

Love leaving distant shadows I turn and you are following me,
Enigmatic friend you appear from ivory mists swirling ahead,
When I need you most you are all around shrouded in mystery,
My very being always bewitched arms reaching I follow your tread.

Jim Wilson

Thoughts Of Love

As I walk amongst the early morning dew,
My mind wanders and I think of you,
As I walk in the early morning mist,
I think of you and when we last kissed,
The sun breaks through and the sky is light,
I think of you and a love that's right,

As I walk in the afternoon sun,
I think of you and know my life has begun,
As I walk and the shadows fall,
I love you for you've given me all,
As I walk in the pale moonshine,
I thank the Lord that you at last are mine,

As I go to my bed to sleep,
I've a smile on my face, no need to weep,
As I lay there and close my eyes,
I feel like I've won a Lottery prize,
I fall asleep and dream of you.
Of the day when you and I will be two,
I love you very, very much,
Everything you do, say and especially your touch.

Malcolm Walker

Aspects Of Love

Under the horses we kissed our first hello
I didn't know which way to go
You made me high when I was low
That's when I knew
I needed you.

In the park, we dreamed our lunch away
We knew exactly what to say
We were in touch in every way
That's when I knew
I felt for you.

When we lay close and kissed by the sea
No one else, just you and me
I first felt love and ecstasy
That's when I knew
I wanted you.

In the night when you stared and began to cry
I'd hold you tight and wonder why
We're here now and there's no goodbye
That's when I knew
I cared for you.

We laughed, we really didn't have to try
My every cell was on a high
Our laughter soared into the sky
That's when I knew
I loved you.

That night when you said you had to go
I never knew I wanted more
But when you finally closed that door
That's when I knew
I'd just lost you.

Andrew Seymour

Father's Memories

Pussy sleeping on the rug
Puppy by her side
Baby begging for a hug
Chubby arms held wide.

Twilight fills the cosy room
Father nods his head
Mother stares into the gloom
Eyes filled with tears unshed.

Gently gently close the door
On the pictures in my mind
Scenes I cherish from before
My seeing eyes came blind.

Do not pity me my dears
The memories last forever
Though sight is gone I have no fears
Our love will leave me never.

Do not weep for me I pray
Though days all seem like nights
Your love will help to show the way
And be my guiding light.

Grace Wallace

Cloth Ears

This world is full of humankind
Who all say that they'll listen;
Such tragedy for those of us
Trapped in our soundproof prison.

How deafening the silent screams
That echo through our fear,
When dawns the mind that those beyond
Don't wish our voice to hear.

Linda Zulaica

Lost Stitches, Lost Youth

There she was, sagging in her chair,
Like a withered potato,
With thin grey hair.
She glanced at the calendar, unaware of the day,
February 14th. She then looked away.

Her head dropped to her chest,
The knitting to the floor,
Her spirit became twenty,
As it danced through the door . . .

As the postman rode by,
On his boneshaker bike,
He tossed her the mail and saw her delight.
Three fancy cards from three different lads,
Jack, Arthur, Fred, all scared of her dad.

She was as fresh as a strawberry,
With curly blonde tresses,
And she twirled in the favourite of all of her dresses.
A shaft of bright sunlight caught a glint in her eye,
Soon to be dulled by a dark winter sky.

She awoke with a start,
And encountered the truth,
Picked up her knitting,
Lost stitches, lost youth.

Ben Springett

Memories

It's a long time since I met you
When you waltzed into my life
We've had many years of married bliss
Since I became your wife
I remember walking down the aisle
All radiant in white
Thinking as I took each step
Was I doing right?
Then I saw you standing there
You looked so young and kind
I knew inside my heart right then
I wouldn't change my mind.
As time passed by our numbers grew
And so did all the bills
But through it all our love survived
With the help of headache pills.
But now at last we're on our own
The kids have flown the nest
I thank the Lord for all he's done
For we are truly blessed.

Rita Smith

SHINE

You made me, make
Me
Glimmer, shine
For one tiny aspect,
A sentence in my mind, a line.
But you're just a stranger,
Another passenger of time.

Kim Stretton

SPARE HIS BLUSHES

He can mend the spin drier, the iron and fire,
And flatten the curved frying pan.
He can straighten my specs and bind a frayed flex,
He's my wizardly, gadgety man!

The sewing machine needs some oil in its spleen
And the hoover is coughing out smoke,
And the cooker door's loose and the tap's dripping juice:
I must really get hold of my bloke.

My mixer for cakes is a tale on its own
He serviced it many a year
Then it finally spluttered and came to a stop
'You've worn the thing out, Sheilah dear.'

'There are limits you know, in how far I can go,
In mending equipment - so hop
And take up your brolly and your shopping trolley
And buy a new one at the shop.'

I'll certainly mention that super invention -
His pen-knife, the tool of his trade.
It's always at hand and in constant demand,
It puts other tools in the shade.

So have you got a clock that is gaining a bit?
Or a teapot whose lid is not straight?
Has the lock on your door developed a flaw?
Or the hinges gone wrong on your gate?

Have you got a fire with the elements gone?
Or is ice freezing up your waste pipe?
Then send for the Vicar - he'll do the job quicker -
You can pay him in onions and tripe ! (His favourite dish.)

Sheilah Upton

My Valentine - My Wife

Oh, the battle-axe is swinging and you'd better watch your neck!
Or you'll very soon be singing 'What has struck me to the deck?'
And the whirlwind is a-whirring, and the storm is rising high;
Your defences must be stirring, or you'll get a big black eye.
The witch's broom is beating, she's preparing for a flight,
So you'd better be retreating to avoid a dreadful fight.

Ah, the battle-axe has rested, and the whirlwind's had its fling,
The storm is now arrested - no witch is on the wing.
The calm is elevating, and peace falls from above,
The strife is now abating, and the time had come for *love*.

Roy Upton

My Deepest Love

My deepest love is sweet and true
It stretches far and wide.
My deepest love depends on you
In love I will abide.

You change my heart, I see new light
For this I live today.
I'll hold this love with all my might
To hear myself once say.

My deepest love, my deepest love
I will not deprave.
I'll take you to the skies above
In you I shall be brave.

My love, my joy and rapture
It's only you I seek.
Your heart I long to capture
Without you I am weak.

Oh love, you are a tale
That reaches high above.
The oceans I will sail
You are my deepest love.

James Lunan

Reborn

Is he that prejudiced young man
I knew years ago as an arrant racist?

Yes, here comes that arrogant young man
Who used to shout at black people
Without rhyme or reason
And hated them all.

For years I had not seen him
And I had almost forgotten him
Until now.
But, then, who is the young woman
He is holding in his arms?

A black girl she is,
Yes, she is black . . . a black beauty!
And I see them,
Look there, right before our eyes,
Hugging and kissing each other!
Can you believe that?

Dear God! So, that is the magic of love!
Love, the leveller, has caused
The death of a downright racist
And the birth of a philanthropist!

S M Tajul Islam

Untitled

Bewitching in your stardom
Glistening smile to all
Except for he who's waiting
Out the back and down the hall
He's been there years it seems, he's sure, on solid ground.
You have given him but tinsel, and the run around.
Don't cry now lady your mascara will run.
Don't sigh now lady, you're having so much fun.

Alluring in your mid years
Popular and more
Except for he who took you
When you were none at all.
He's there it seems for love, no less, love of that deeper sort.
Well two can play at loving dear, you loved around - for sport.
Don't try now lady, you may lose out on fame.
Don't give up now lady, you've so much left to gain.

The razz, the tazz all over now
The music jaded, low.
Here's he who remembers waiting,
Out the back, so long ago.
He's been there years, with dreams. He's sure, on solid ground
While all he got was tinsel, and the run around.
With toothless chin, and shingles, white powdered cheeks and jaw,
He knows that now he's got you, and he loves you all the more.

Barbara Steward

THE DISTANCE BETWEEN US

My soul cringes within me when the receiver is replaced.
All of those words and comments babbled in haste.
Not one mention or even a hint that I love you.
Therefore this poem is written to assure you that I do.

We need to remember why we fell in love.
Our great sense of humour and our burning ambitions,
Even though the distance between us puts us in an awkward position.

It is hard not sharing my present life with you.
I want to phone you each evening to discuss my news.
We need to be positive and live our lives to the full,
not sit by the phone waiting for a call.

We are intelligent people, but have plenty to learn.
We need strength and determination to keep us from drifting apart,
if our love flourishes, it should not be too hard.

Other people should always be relevant in our lives,
to laugh with and to keep us occupied.
As long as we both know who is number one,
then communication between us should be quite fun.

Meaningful, loving letters, or postcards that are short and sweet,
can keep our love growing if they are sent each week.
I love you Richard,
and I hope this poem helps to bridge the gaps,
that we manage to create after unsuccessful chats.

Kelly Simpson

VALENTINE'S DAY

Valentine's Day
A time to say
How much we care,
To get fruity if you dare.
I want to let you know,
To let my feelings flow,
Write it all out on the page.
Be big and bold like an actor on a stage.
I love you
And lust for you too.
Dream about you,
And the things you do;
Clean and dirty,
Innocent and flirty,
I love you beyond Valentine's Day
What more can I say.

Chris Wagg

WHISPERS OF LOVE

Whispers of love
fall from heaven above.
Whispers of love
my name, they call
heard in a waterfall
as it cascades down.
Whispers of love
a seed gently sown
deep within my heart
growing from the start.
Whispers of love
carried swiftly by the breeze
travelling across the seas.
Whispers of love
all over the land
drifting along the sands.
Whispers of love
we can find
in hands entwined.
Whispers of love
in dark of night
and dawning light.
Whispers of love
carried on wings of a dove.
Whispers of love
blow through the trees.
Forever running free.
Whispers of love
they gently sigh
until eternity, for you and I.

Elaine Hicklin

When Mother Died, Aged 88 (A Day In June 1995)

I sat with her, not knowing if she knew,
This wisp of cancer-claimed humanity.
I stroked her brow, ran fingers through her hair,
Thin white hair, once thick auburn, now all frailty.

I didn't know the things I should have said,
Until the time to say them was long past.
I took for granted she would somehow know
But was I right? I hope so, at the last.

The room was hot, a strange, warm early June,
She liked the place we'd found for her to die.
With grief, I felt she couldn't understand;
She never ceased her sickness to deny.

Throughout her life her evening prayers she said,
And now 'Our Father' whispered in a sigh,
'I have so much to do!' I crumbled then.
I held her close. I prayed, 'What help am I?'

Life slipped away more softly than a sigh;
The peace of God alighted on her face,
A blackbird's silver vesper to the sky
Soothed all the earthly sadness from the place.

A fitting escort for her spirit's flight,
The bird took wing in evening's fading light.

Marjorie Tetlow

MEG

Those dear brown eyes so strong and
full of love
hold my gaze.
I smile because you understand
my every thought,
my every feeling.
You dance and pirouette
to share my joy.
You sit quietly and are always
there in my grief.
You are tolerant and forgiving
in my darkest moods.
My dearest friend, your
love is unconditional -
Do I deserve so much?
You give your affection so selflessly
and ask for nothing in return,
except to share my company
in the fresh air
and the miles upon miles of
silent contemplation.
My dearest friend,
I'll never walk alone in this dismal
depressing world,
never be sad when I see the constantly
wagging tail.
Meg - you are simply the
best.

Judith Vale

SCENT

The pain grows deeper
Rain beats upon the window
His name, his presence
His scent, deeper and deeper.

Jeanette Wilkes

SAM

Quite simply, it was a love affair,
I found him, quite by chance;
He stood in a field, tall and still,
His feathers waving in the wind.
He shone, like a bronzed statue,
His chestnut coat, glistening in the morning sun.
A red setter.
He bounded towards me, my heart was captured.
Slim, elegant like a tiny horse;
He was the most beautiful creature.

Pamela Stoner

LOVE

Love is something we can't do without
Of that, most of us have no doubt
Now I was happily married until one day
When death took my dear husband away.

Now having no family I was on my own
In every way
I missed my husband more every day
I felt so lonely all alone every day
If I hadn't friends, what would I say.

Then one day a friend died and left
Her husband so sad,
I tried to help him I knew he'd be glad
He'd come when lonely often to see me
And very often he'd stay to tea.

Time went really very fast
And suddenly we knew we were in love at last
We couldn't forget our old loves in any way
But knew love for each other had to stay.

Now I have children which gives me joy
Doesn't matter if they're girl or boy
The children are so good and kind
Never thought I'd have such love in kind.

I even have great grandchildren
Which I love
It seems they were sent from Heaven above
My heart is really full of joy
At the moment they are all boys.

So love is certainly the best part of life
Whatever your worry or your strife
The joy stepchildren brought me
Is there for everyone to see.

We hope the Lord in Heaven above
Takes care of those we loved.

K Taylor

If You Love Me, Jilt The Gossips

Neighbourhood opinion, be
Damned! Spurn its ignominy -
As I do, and love me, now.
Neither you nor I should care how
Cups of happiness were dashed
From those talkers, who have smashed.

Other lovers' joy with malice.
Envy's venom sours the chalice.
Pride and a good name are lonely
Assets, gained from nights with only
Company of unkissed lips!
Just ignore their jaundiced quips.

Gillian Fisher

A Rose

The rose my
Prose
Cannot convey
All blushing
At the close
Of day.
He the master
Fashioned them
To bloom
Live love
Eternally.

David A Bray

LOVE'S LUST

Two loves I have, one counterfeit called lust.
Love slowly grows, and lasts a lifetime long.
But lust, once felt, is instant and more strong -
A quenchless quest for gold that turns to dust.
Love cares and is compassionate and just:
Lust only seeks its own, however, wrong.
Love suffers, and would selflessly belong:
Lust cheats and kills, risks all to win or bust.

Yet love swears but to love till death do part,
And when life ends the lover's vows will waive:
Lust, all unsatisfied and wracked of heart,
Tortures itself and clings beyond the grave.

Who is more constant then? He who loves well,
Or he who would pursue his love to Hell?

Bernard Brown

Bumpity Bump

Drifting through life, touched by the thrill of love,
I have travelled down that road too often,
When an ending is in sight, pain,
Heartache and many tears follow;
Yet, remembering the joy of love,
The passions and intensity it reveals,
I weaken again, when it reappears,
Sparkling eyes, smiles exchanged,
Bumpity-bump as the heart races.

Meetings ensue, romantic whispers on the telephone,
Promises of undying love are made,
The images of each, become a flawless perfection,
Crushing any defect before it comes into existence.
Magical, bewitching times, when each only wants to please,
Showering the other with gifts and affection.
Bumpity-bump as Heaven's door opens wide.

The spell has been cast and the anticipations,
Are nurtured into a reality that possesses each of them;
Nothing holds any importance, only the commitment made,
The foundations seem rock hard,
Time is left behind, as each waits for a brand new day,
Talking, loving and learning more about the other.
Bumpity-bump, missing him, wondering why he is late.

Excuses made, when he apologises over the phone,
Your heart sinks, you haven't seen him for three days,
Tediously time passes. And truth makes an entrance.
The years have moved on, so has he, but he forgot to tell you;
You pick yourself up and struggle through each day,
Slowly you begin to realise, there is life after love,
Convinced you can live without it, you discover you were wrong.
Bumpity-bump . . .

Amanda-Lea Manning

THE BOY I LOVE

Every Tuesday I see you,
Just for the past three weeks,
My love for you is so true.
Your love for me I seek.

I am with you for two whole hours,
When you come to Heddon-on-the-Wall,
You're so sweet you'd even pick me flowers.
You're older than me but you are so small.

You come to my house,
If you're going to pick me up,
You're hardly as quiet as a mouse.
When I come to yours I get a drink in a cup.

We do karate for one hour,
We always partner together,
We put in strength and power.
I will love you forever.

I cannot tell you his name,
His comedy gives him his fame,
Being so sweet is his game.
But I love him all the same.

Then one day he asked me out,
All of my dreams had come true,
I was ready to scream and shout,
All the waiting is now through.

Michelle McMahon

Buffy's Angel

Even though demons rule our lives, surfacing only when we are weak,
I love you more today, than my memories of yesterday.
For just a moment in time, in my heart you'll always be mine.
Cos even when you're gone, my heart still sings your song.
A beautiful symphony of everything that you are to me.
Like an angel's choir, you're all that I desire
Within a clock's chime, it's a love on borrowed time.
Cos we can never be sure, of all that we adore,
When life changes the scene of where love has been,
So remember this, like our very first kiss
You made me live, through the love that you did give.

Amanda Jayne Biro

Lundy Island

The scent of the bracken comes wafting to meet me,
As I climb the dunes in the evening light,
Lundy Island, dark shape on horizon,
Her beacons flashing, the jewels of night.

The sun sinks slowly o'er the far side of Lundy,
Imparting a deep fiery glow to the sky,
Touched with flame are the incoming waters
Of the vast Atlantic, the tide running high.

Out on the shoreline, an army of seagulls,
Like patient sentinels, wait on the sand,
High above them the grey clouds, pink breasted,
Are paint-splashed by Nature's voluptuous hand.

The scent of the bracken comes wafting to meet me,
As I climb the dunes in the evening light,
Lundy Island, dark shape on horizon,
Her beacons flashing, the jewels of night.

Monni Aldous

Time Out

Though we are thirty-four we were eighteen
the air tremulous with expectation
the air fresh and honeyed as
the first spring day we could ever remember
yet we were indoors it was winter and dark

we were breathless and awed in the shimmering silence
we were together alone we could touch
we could breathe each other's breath we were astounded
overwhelmed by a multitude of pleasure suddenly ours.

I drank in the room desperately before leaving
so I could remember could always picture you there
but all I ever could recall was the dark
your silhouette breathless stillness and wonder

Now the many years since you and then
prove the unspoken equation that was to be the only time
divest of everyday clothes everyday roles
the nerves of our being laid bare our souls in touch
we paused for truth in the lie of our lives.

Gail Davis

Treasured Love

In history there's never been
A better man found
No God or King ever seen
That deserved your crown
Body fitting for the throne
Bronzed, a perfect mould
Eyes as blue as precious stones
Hair of flowing gold
Lips as warm as amber pressed
Smile full of pearls
With all the jewels that you possess
You could win any girl
Some day the one will be found
Who will hold the key
That opens up your treasure trove
I hope she will be me.

Amanda Shakesby

Carrie

Your petals
So gentle
Velvet like
Rapturous colour
So bright.

Your scent
So sweet
Strawberry like
Distinctly unique
Such a treat.

Your heart
So warm
Incomparable like
Open or closed
Cautions thorns
Protect this rose.

Your company
So absorbing
Sponge like
Soothing serenity
Mental agility.

You, your ways
You, your days
You, I bay
For some time, for some moments
For yours, for mine
For all our cares
Let us lay here
Thoughts and feelings
Bare.

Kristopher Thurbin

Beloved

There is none like you
No one else can touch my heart like you do
In the stolen moments we share
Your love keeps me warm
I reach the heights, ride on the clouds
Marvel, in awe of you
Like a feather that returns to the earth gliding on a gentle breeze
I'm swept up in the magic of your touch
And I never want you to put me down
Hold me, in the shelter of your wings
Wrap me up safe and warm
Love me, your name is like honey on my lips
My knight in shining armour
Rescues me from all those who try to bring me harm
And my face so dear, so precious to you
Engraved in the palm of your hand
Etched on the forefront of your mind
Forever mine
And I
Forever your beloved.

Darlene Skeete

FAREWELL KISS

Your lips are warm to the touch,
You make me want you oh! so much.
You reawaken memories of youth
And bring back words of truth.
Those gentle lips bathe in mine,
Their moisture tastes of summer wine.
My pulse races at great speed
For, of you, I have a need.
The passions of my inner soul
Make my head spin and roll
Until I faint upon the floor,
So frail now and very poor.

So gently take me to your breast,
Then carefully lay me down to rest.
Stroke my trembling hands and say
All the things you never said today
Nor will think or speak again,
For I am fading with the pain.
My senses lessen, my time draws nigh
Soon our entangled knot will untie.

My heart grows weak -
I cannot speak
The air is being sucked away
And I can no longer stay.
My breath grows weak inside of me,
My eyes dim, I cannot see.
Let me once more your lips take,
Just one kiss for old times' sake.
Grant me one magical moment of bliss -
One last and lingering, farewell kiss.

Jane Anita Webber

What You Mean To Me?

I may not often tell you how
much you mean to me,
You are my life, my rock,
my love and my stability.

When times are hard,
when I am blue and sad,
You take my hand, you
hold me tight,
suddenly, things do not seem
so bad.

I cannot ever imagine a life,
without you by my side,
I would feel empty, bereft,
so lonely inside.

My dearest love,
I want to be with you forever,
Caring for you, cherishing you,
As we tread life's path together.

Linda Kathleen Harker

A Whispered Caress

Love: love is vital . . . o la la
love is nutritious nourishment
love makes the person live struggle strive
in peace peacefully
in every moment everyday's
kaleidoscopic lives living
and whisper . . . even cry . . . loud and clear
can I call you sweetheart . . . may I consider you sweetheart
we have one thing in common
you are a woman . . . I am a man
to unite in unison . . . to form a couple
to create the next generation
with our symbol of love
to continuation of mankind
I know there are reasons
not to accept me
as a partner till death us do part
you are a beautiful woman
with financial resources
I am a handsome man struggling
this creates a barrier
but we can overcome it all together
the magic band of love will do it all
try it let us believe and imitate
the initial point of marriage
a married couple life . . . o! life . . . o! life . . .

Ghazanfer Eqbal

. . .AND THE WORLD SLIPS AWAY

I leave the world, tired and
worn, senses jagged and torn.
And there's your smile behind
the waiting door and
a welcome in your heart; and I
step into your arms, stay
locked so, until the world
slips away and we
are one smile, one heart
that all the cares
of the years shall never part.

Jocelyn McKinnon

SO LOVED

No mater what I've done
No matter what I do
There's nowhere I can run
To hide away from you
My rock of constancy
Faithful and steadfast God
I know I'll always be
- So loved.

So loved, that You would die for me
So loved, a Son to set me free
Jesus, that you'd do this for me
And now I'm - so loved.

You search me deep within
Knowing my thoughts, my deeds
The frailty and the sin
Seeing my every need
Yet grace and mercy flow
Pouring from precious blood
So that I always know
- I'm so loved.

Debbie Trewhella

IF ONLY

Careless words like raindrops fall
Sadly each one I recall
In memory they'll always stay
Tears will not wash them away
Oh to have that day again
And the moments of before
Ev'ry word chose carefully
Who could ask for more?
No sleepless nights
No heavy heart
Just joy and happy days
A future bright
From morn till night
If we could mend our ways.

Maureen Tooze

FRUITS OF SUMMER

My heart
            bursting to taste
sunny nectarines
            sweet to the lips
cherries
            rich juice like blood
warm velvet
            roundness
and touches of you

I kiss the lids that close
over the polished curves
of your sleeping amber eyes
dazzling in daylight
hidden and guarded at night

I watch you
caught in a shaft of silver light
still as a child feigning sleep
and am amazed
again
at all this summer's sweetness
magically distilled
            in you.

A Slade

The Night-Watchman's Vigil

Way past midnight
cold wet black
A solitary figure
by the railway track

Last train whaled by
over an hour since
Light from a window
a solitary glimpse

A reply from the figure
flickers into night
At first dull yellow
then ominous white

Held low his lantern's
yellow ominous glow
Falls into a doorway
open to the snow

He draws up to the doorway
a cautious half stumble
Whispers into the night
a stutter half mumbled

No, they won't be home tonight
his mumbled half mutter
Dowse the candle
put out the light
His lantern spat and spluttered

As his lantern spat
I thought I heard him say
God bless our children
wherever they are today

The light put out
he drew upright
His lantern spat out
the door shut tight

Then I turning
began to walk away
As the sun slowly rose
On to Christmas Day

R J Collins

SHE

Where is she
what's she on
can't communicate
her mind's gone

Once out there, sharp and astute
substance abuse, she can't cope
caught now on a spiral route
what end - what hope

Out of her head
from waking eyes
saddened and red
can't see her cries

Rambling thoughts and mumbled word
tumbling out, never heard
what now, we wait to see
who cares? does she . . .

Kimberley An Balaam

THESE THINGS I MISS

A reflection in a shop window
A shadow on the wall
A tinkle of a wind chime
Remind me of you
The smell of blossom blowing
Through sunny windswept days
The seagulls on the harbour
The canvas flapping wild
The sound of distant music
The crashing of the tide
A roller-coaster roaring
High above my head
The screaming from the ghost train
A walk along the pier
These things I miss so dearly
How I wish that you were here

Michael Tarbox

Around The Last Bend

This old hand now shakes,
as I climb into bed.
I lay down beside you,
and think of the love unsaid.

Our years have gone,
so quickly past;
and I'm sorry now,
that I did not cast.

My love more deeply,
into your heart and soul.
For in the twilight of my years,
I want to be whole.

I want to be whole,
and love you once more.
The way I used to,
when we stood on life's shore.

But now I stand,
where the waters end.
Where God awaits me,
around the last bend.

So my love I leave you,
for I've come to my life's end.
But I'll wait for you forever,
around the last bend.

Eve Schmidt

The Heart Aches

Here, breaths only emerge as sighs.
My heart is sinking with the weight of your absence.
It is trying to cope with your love and beauty.
With each short breath and unfocused stare,
It thuds in the soles of my shoes, they will turn back to you.

The kitchen clock consists of cogs and springs.
They work together to remind me that only four minutes
Have passed since I last looked.
Persuading them that I do not want your touch to fade,
The pressure of your kiss to fade, tires me.
Your echo cushions me as I wade into the clotted slowness of sleep
That captures the innocence of us all.

Deep, sweet night slumber.
Discussing the purpose of starfish.
A mumbled bumble plummeting in a muffled fumble.
The essence of the protection of angels.
Against the face,
The air whisked by the furious wing of a hummingbird.
Snug forgetfulness before lavish swoons of soothing caresses.
Playing as one in a field of euphoria, enveloped in Him.
Ten thousand clouds visit unexpectedly.
A nocturnal flight on a dragonfly, topping an expunged swamp.

Light folds into the restful pillow.

Daylight insists me into its plan and the stark sun tests love,
Even beyond dreams . . . it passes.
Step, blink, heartbeat.
Each is enriched by the night's tapestry that weaves the noon.

The kitchen clock remains over stale toast and cold coffee
And finds this man even deeper in love with you.
It shall do so tomorrow, my sweet,
And even more shall you.

Damion Sizer

A Love Undying

A love undying,
Ever strengthening
And always understanding.

A love that forgives and forgets easily,
That never lets you down,
Never abandons you.

A love made strong in its pain,
In its sacrifice,
In its suffering.

A love pure and selfless,
Ever secure, never to fade,
A love, Lord, only you can give!

N Yogaratnam

A Rose

A rose, their sign, signalling new
A future to lean upon each clue
Its scent is fresh upon her face
From skin to heart covered by lace

Serene, webbed by pink and white
Shining brightly in sundance light
Revealing images of intricate design
He follows her beauty to every line

She's cool, showing her loving care
Smoothing in mutual wanting to share
In melting times of mellowed embrace
Past is continued in following trace

To where lost hearts finally meet
Under colonnades of truth they greet
Walking in time and space to devour
Beauty encompassed in love's flower

Rob Tapley

Love's Whisper

Your name is whispered on wings of love,
Your eyes are seen in the blue sky above,
Your hair is remembered in a blackbird's wing
Your touch and embrace are remembered -
When I see your face.

When you ask -
'What is that look in your eyes?'
You're looking at 'love' - no disguise,
But, you are looking thro a veil -
So my love for you is to no avail!

It lives on in my mind and heart uninvited,
The kind of love that is unrequited!

Aileen Andrews

Frozen Without Reason

My luck has run out
I must now face the music,
There is no one to love
I now have to dance.

I am missing the beat
My mind has no action,
My body won't function
My walk has no bounce.

I cannot raise my head
And my arms cannot swing,
My heart and soul are dead
And my voice, a note, can't sing.

I am now an object of disfunction
And the energy source has burned me down,
I am lame from so much burden
That slowly lays me to the ground.

I now sleep astride a grave
And such guilt makes me believe,
That this for me is happier
Than what was thought.

But while I am a sleeping beauty
Mannequined and medused to stone,
I'll lie in silent anger
Until my switch is caught.

Samantha Watt

EVERGREEN

Moss by a wall, a fairy's couch
Soft, plush, velvet and green,
With just a hint of pink.

Soft and full as your mouth,
As we took our first kiss
On a warm summer evening in June,
Lingering and tender,
With all the sweetness of youth.
For we were but nineteen.

Yet in our callow maturity,
Knew that this would last.
Last like the moss in the cleft of that dark wall.

We clung to each other over the years,
Clung to the advent of that time
While keeping our own coalescence
Until, with that sharp death at an early age,
One of us had to depart.

But you are there,
In the thought of our first greeting,
Tall, shy, fair and bronzed.

And though the years have gone between,
Still the song of our first meeting,
Is like the moss,
Mysterious and evergreen,
The lichen of our souls entwined.

Mary Ling

MOTHERS

Mothers are not just someone,
There for all our needs.
Mothers, are very special,
One's greatest friend indeed.

They're there through all the
Good times.
There, throughout the bad.
They, are that special someone,
Who can make you smile when sad.

Can cheer you up.
Make you feel good.
Lets you know you're special too.
Even thought you've forgotten to call,
Or say, Mum, I love you.

So Mum, this verse is for you.
And now, I can't find the words to say,
All the things I'd like to.
So I'll say it in the simplest of ways.

Mum, you're so very special.
Loved, very much in every way.
Mum, thank you from the heart,
Today, and always.

Valerie Gwenllian Wall

WHISPERED WORDS OF LOVE

So fascinating is your whispered love
Into my tender ear
Uttered by my gentle beau towering above
Me, whispering sweet nothings
How wonderful to hear
Intimate expressions bearings
Of constant desire and an everlasting loving cove
Hug me until I feel inside a blazing fire
Kindling within my heart
Whispered words of love
Tingle and linger with heavenly feelings
My words of whispered love whispered in your ear
Will always be, I worship you,
You are my most treasured possession
I will adore you for ever and ever

Alma Montgomery Frank

A Whispered Caress

You call to me deep within
I hear your call and I give in
To float in misty seas of love
To feel your touch a velvet glove
To know that all you say is true
Makes me want to call to you

Ruth Hughes

AUTUMN LOVE

Oh, what perfect wondrous bliss
Since tasting that first gentle kiss.
Instead of feeling winter's chill
I only feel the magic thrill.
No icy wind on fingertips
Just your warm breath upon my lips.

That burnished gold of autumn glow
Shall not succumb to winter's snow.
You've turned my autumn into spring
With feelings only love can bring;
You put the leaves back on the trees
And daffodils where only grass should be.

No more will autumn come and go
To be replaced by wind and snow.
Instead that tapestry of bronze and gold
Will live right on through all the cold:
Until at last spring bursts on through,
Just like our love to start anew.

Norman Watson

EPITHALAMIUM ON ISAAC AND REBEKAH COMING TOGETHER

Abraham's faith calls out a spouse for Isaac;
Providence hears and forms this thing of the *Lord.*
'Wilt thou go with this man, Rebekah my beloved daughter
Which knows not a Man?'
'I will go.'

Two score Isaac prays, and waits, and meditates;
Young Rebekah and the joyous host enters his field.
'Wilt thou go with this man, Rebekah my beloved daughter
Which knows not a Man?'
'I will go.'

Rebekah espies, dismounts, heart burning speaks;
'Who is this man walking in the field to meet us?'
'Wilt thou go with this man, Rebekah my beloved daughter
Which knows not a Man?'
'I will go.'

Dean Stevenson

A Whispered Caress

From Him
My ears heard
And body felt the sweetness
Of a whispered caress
I could feel
His breath upon my face
Gently he said I'm sorry
Whilst we stood locked together
In a warm embrace
Our eyes met and held a while
Then I watched his look of relief
As he noticed my smile
When you love
You forgive and forget
For true love
Has no harbour for bitterness or regret
Softly he said I've missed you
We laughed about old times
Then sat and talked things through
Quietly I said
Everything will be just fine
In the spell of the moment
His lips found mine
Our hearts were reunited with happiness
And as he turned to leave
I heard a whispered caress.

Joan Taylor

A Symbol Of Love

There's a symbol of love in the garden
In the form of a beautiful rose
Every petal is shaped to perfection
Its beauty excels as it grows.

It's been handled with care by the grower
So lovingly nurtured and bred,
Gently splashed by the dew and the raindrops
A vision of soft velvet red.

For a lover to give to his sweetheart
Such a token would light up her face,
And what bliss in that wonderful bouquet
For the bride with her chiffon and lace.

If placed by the bed in a sick-room
The patient would perk up anew,
And displayed with the flowers on the altar
Its reverence would come shining through.

It holds pride of place in the garden
A picture for all to behold,
A graceful and fragrant creation
With the message of love it enfolds.

F Evelyn D Jones

I HATE TO SEE YOU HURT

I hate to see you hurt
You are wounded easily
Like the daffodil
In a blustery shower
Once tall and copious
The next moment
Bent to the ground
Unable even to show her tears
The slightest memory of an ill wind
Turns your head, shades your looks
Your only answer to treachery
Is disbelief and
Darkness
For there is no shining steel in your defence
No bright eyed tempest
And yet you would temper a challenge
And turn a heart, my heart, to remorse
If by thoughtless deed
You were dismayed
Only
I hate to see you hurt
Your wounds may heal
May not show
But you carry a burden of cruelty
Which, like the daffodils
Is whispered to the earth,
I would rather you
Whispered it to me.

Richard Smythe

Out Of The Blue

. . . watching the moon rise,
thinking of a new love - hardly
regarded on the bare edge
of consciousness.
. . . a shadow-glimpse, then
fading, against the haze of evening.
. . . plane-lights came flashing,
signalling the night-fall - blotting
out the moon shape behind the still
trees.
. . . pallid marshmallow
edges blurred by mist; then blushing,
soared.
. . . complete refulgent
globe, released from earth's vapours
to ride the night sky,
. . . a gift unsought brings forth
a love now known.

Alisoun M Ward

WHO'S WHO

You are,
My eyes that see
My voice that speaks
My ears that listen
My heart that beats
My mind that thinks
My senses that be
To all intent and purpose
You might as well be me.

Michael Gardner

REPINING

I said I'd stop regretting,
The things I did, or didn't do,
But in my hours of loneliness
My thoughts are all with you.

I think of all the chances missed
To show my love for you,
I'm sad I did not realise
How much you loved me too.

With so much time to sit and think:
. . . I was too busy then . . .
My heart is sore with longing
That we could try again.

But there are no second chances,
I've learnt that much too late.
Perhaps there are, in *Heaven*
So, in *hope* and *peace* I'll wait.

Kathleen Warneken

For What Love Is Worth

Your heart is the essence encased in my soul
Your eyes are padlocked forever in my mind
Your presence excited me; so I am inclined
To love you forever even if the love is blind

Don't be disheartened by wrong gestures or moves
Don't think love is stuck in a deep endless groove
Don't give up your feelings, believe what is true
Be happy with love and it will be happy with you

Possessed by dreams of frequent occasion
Amongst an atmosphere in which love can flourish
Scared hearts get stuck in an ore of confusion
Instead of this let our love be encouraged

Times can prove hard through jealous minds
Picking up the pieces whenever we can find
And instead of fun and laughter we cry
As yellow candles burn profligately against a blackened sky

Forget old tales of anguish and despair
Forget stale love lingering in savage air
Enjoy the now and the love we feel
For the future brings us onto an eventual even keel

J L Hammond

OUR LOVE

Our love it has no boundary
Our love it has no ends
Our love is ours to cherish
Our love on life depends
Our love can conquer over
Our love can overthrow
Because our love can never end
This we both do know

Graham Smith

Love Me Forever

Take me to your heart let me hear that old refrain
Press your lips close to mine and the sweetness will remain
Help me climb the mountains till we reach the highest peak
Don't hold back the tide of love too full for us to speak
Hold your love save your love give it all to me
Treasure it for always keep it in your memory
In my heart there lives an image I carry with me still
No one can replace it no one ever will
Please don't fail me it's you I adore
Magic are the moments that we will share once more
As long as grass stays green and there is salt in the sea
And birds are still singing there is hope for you and me.

Barbara Tunstall

If I Was A Tree

What if I was a tree
spreading my leaves to the sun
enticing you -
how many times would you climb me
to pick my summer fruit?

And what when the autumn comes
and the summer fruit is done -
what then?

Would you gather my leaves
and fire them
on some neglected land?

And what of the ashes -
what of them?

Would you spread them about my roots
or would you let the wind
carry them off -
to eternal blight?

L Simcock-Daisy

WHISPERS

The leaves on the trees
whispering together,
as the wind flows through,
the singing of the birds,
the hum of the bees,
flying from flower to flower.
The dancing of the maiden,
by the water's edge,
the sweet voice of a song,
flowing from her lips,
of red wine, the shape
of a heart, and a kiss
of a kiss, whisper of a sound.

Olive Irwin

TRUE LOVE CONQUERS ALL

Those chemical reactions
That spell love
They give satisfaction
The ones that are woven
What are the symptoms
That create happiness
A tender moment being an item
A warm soothing kiss.

Apply your reflexes
And together yield
Only for the two sexes
Who are fed up playing the field
Love conquers all
Truly in first gear
So both walk tall
Year by year.

Bless teenagers and adults too
First or second time
When hearts are subdued
This moment is sublime
It's no mistake to caress
And show kindness
And in return
both hearts blessed.

Love tingles
Love shakes
Go to the singles
Give yourself a break
Hail joy end despair
Whisper love that is not rare.

John Sneddon

Real You

And finally now I'm ready,
to face the world on my own.
Thank you for your hand, I'm steady,
I can manage all alone.

I still have a lot to learn,
no need to explain to me.
On my heels I can now turn,
and you've given me your key.

I've put emotions on the shelf,
I now know just what to do.
I have finally found myself,
but I've found the real you.

My everyday angel, you are,
Without your light I was at a loss.
Your guidance has become my star,
I am now my own boss.

The lessons to me you teach,
on how to get by.
Cope with this world, to reach,
even help to cry.

If you weren't by my side,
I don't know where I'd be.
Alone in a world that lied,
you'll always be next to me.

Jamie Barnes

Red Rose Of Perfection

I send you a rose
with my love and affection
to show you in my heart,
I send you a rose
of perfect perfection
a symbol of love that we did start,
I send you a rose
with true love and emotion
a rose to pledge my devotion.

I P Smyth

My Love

Happy Anniversary,
And happy birthday too,
To me there is no other,
As beautiful as you.

Your beauty is not skin deep,
It reaches to your core,
You know you are my everything,
In fact you're even more.

As you know, mere words can't tell,
The way I feel for you,
And neither can mere words express,
The kind of things you do.

I love your little movements,
I love your point of view,
I love your depth of tolerance,
That's only found in few!

I love your tender lips on mine,
I love your sweet embrace,
It makes it so much easier,
To make it through this place!

Andy Shed

On The Red Light

The consummate professional:
Chatting, to put me at my ease.
Gently, he helps me to prepare:
Attentive - deftly prompting then
Questioning - polishing my speech.

And I feel fine: thoughts marshalled, my
Subject sets out in my mind; with
Favourite phrases practised, checked,
I'm eloquent and in control.

'I think we're ready now, he says,
'We're rolling when the red light shows.'

. . . And on the red light thoughts escape,
Eloquence evaporates and
I become a stuttering wreck -
Tongue almost tied.

Always on the
Red light it's the same: confidence
Withers, lines are fluffed, the simplest
Truth stays lodged in my dry throat. And
Always at these times I need my
Best. Instead thick tongued I croak and
Whisper all life's important lines
Like . . . 'I want you, need you, love you.'

Patrick Osada

JUST FOR YOU

This poem I write just for you
So full of love, so kind and true,
Your face it shines with your lovely smile,
I want to dance with you a while.
Let me take you by the hand,
Lead you to the promised land.
I'll buy you roses, a dozen red,
Tuck you safely in your bed.
Kiss your lips with tenderness,
Give you love and happiness.
Dine you in the candlelight,
Hold you closely through the night.
I'll always be there by your side,
Together we can surf the tide.
In the moonlight we will walk,
And words of love we both will talk.
Romance will show how much I care,
As a gentle breeze blows in our hair.
I will hold you in my arms,
Guard you evermore from harm.
I will ease away your pain,
Wait for hours in the pouring rain.
Write you letters sealed with love,
Just for you I would do the things above.
Yes, just for you I'd do all these,
For you're the girl I want to please.

Stephen Martin

Him

He sits and looks straight through me,
As though I am not there.
His flirting drives me crazy,
For me he doesn't care.
One day I will confront him,
Say what I feel inside.
maybe tell him I love him,
For these feelings I just can't hide.
But I'm scared of his reaction,
Whatever it may be.
That's all that I'm afraid of,
For I know that it could hurt me.
So after all I've thought of,
The strong feelings I've had from the start.
He definitely has to know
It's *him* that stole my heart.

Dawn Pettitt (15)

LOVE RAT . . . ROSES AND THORNS . . .

Two double brandies
Coffee for me
What you see
Is what you get
If you get me . . .

French cigarettes
Scarlet lipstick on the end
Bed is beckoning
But you weren't reckoning
What room service would send

Strawberries and champagne
Scented body lotion
Give up the ghost
Give up me
Give up that foolish notion
Eat some toast

Hangover cures . . . hair of the dog
But even the dog
Will pop his clogs
Unless you pop
The question to me

So smartly dressed
Briefcase in hand
Not his usual one night stand
I gave him my card
He gave me his word
A promise is a promise

White satin and lace
Delicately blushing face
He started the love match
And served the ace
But that's alright
As long as he . . .
               . . . knows his place . . .

Sally Wyatt

PRECIOUS LOVE

Oh my dear it doesn't go this pain
inside just grows and grows,
it makes my heart break, to know,
when I awake my love,
your pillow alone is beside me.
I reach out but you're not there,
I call your name out loud in prayer,
I ask for comfort from God above
for he alone understands my love.
My tears have been falling all night through,
I've twisted and turned and also lived through,
the last hours of your life, God in Heaven help me
with my plight, I miss you so much my precious one
I'm trying to be strong, soon the day will come
and once more you'll take me in your arms,
I know that this will be,
but it's the waiting my darling
that's so hard for me.
But I'll wait, yes I'll wait, you're precious
and worth it to me.

Jayne Miles

I LOVE YOU MORE

I love you more than hot kisses on a cold winter's night,
I love you more than the glittering early morning light,
I love you more than the sun and star spangled moon,
I love you more than bright red roses in flaming June,
I love you more than snow and ice,
I love you more than a brilliant sunrise,
I love you more than crispy autumn leaves,
I love you more than an early evening breeze,
I love you more than shining lights at Christmas time,
I love you more because you're mine,
I love you more than frost glistening on a window pane,
I love you more than sweet smelling rain,
I love you more than swans in flight,
I love you more than the pale moonlight,
I love you more than the mouth-watering smell of home-made cake,
I love you more than the silent ripples on a Scottish lake,
I love you more than snowdrops in the early morning dew,
I love you more simply because you're you.

Sally Hunter

LOVE IS

Love is sharing,
Always caring.
Through life's ups and downs,
Through thick and thin,
And in-between,
It never lets you down.

Love is giving,
And also forgiving,
If you're deemed to cast a frown,
When they've done something wrong
Just mend it with this song,
Glad that they're still around.

Love is laughter,
And joy everafter,
Oh: what a heavenly sound
Two hearts entwining
Arms inviting,
Love is all around.

Patricia Taylor

CARIAD

Oh how I loved you, Maggie fach,
In sunshine and in rain,
You, cool and fragrant, light and lithe,
Me, such an awkward swain!

Oh how I worshipped Maggie fach,
The apple of my eye,
Oh how she made me live and laugh,
Oh how she made me cry!

Oh how I missed you, Maggie fach,
Each minute, hour and day,
Oh how I hated Dafydd Price
For taking you away!

Where are you now my Maggie fach?
I loved you, love you dear,
If only I had told you so
When once I held you near!

Peter Davies

LOVE IN SPRINGTIME

A whispered caress
Love can be a breath of spring
Sullen as a thunder cloud
Raising your highest hopes
Just to let you down.

Quickly rushes by
Sometimes never leaving
Takes you to the clouds
Touch the silver lining.

Swift like a bird on the wing
Shines bright silver frost
Elusive patterns sapphire blue
Mysteriously are lost.

True love, brings joy to the heart
Weave your threads around it
Springtime now will start.

What is this magic
The spell that is cast
Makes you feel different
Are you sure it will last?

Dawn is breaking
To start a new day
With spring in your heart
Every step of the way.

Joyce Taylor

CONVERSATION

Not with pen or pencil,
Line of prose or verse,
Can with one another,
All lovers converse.

So it has been ever,
Since the world was round,
Eyes will tell their story,
Hearts will words confound.

Where can we find the Poet,
Who would choose to list,
All that lovers understand,
In a single kiss!

Mary Hughes

Lost Love

I find myself in deep despair
depression fills my heart and soul
when once I was so happy there
my heart was filled with only gold
her hands and head are warm no more
no blushing face and smiling lips as before
she clasps my hand and tries to speak
her breath be stilled her heart is weak
the beauty of her fragile smile
beams up her delicate face
we were together for a while
and held fast in a fond embrace.

Eunice Neale

My Sweet Katey

A day is too long, without you, not hearing or having you near
Dwell constant my thoughts about you, by magic, I wish you'd appear
In circles my mind ever travelling, the theme is ever the same
About a kind and lovely person, sweet Katey, I call her by name.

Bill Vass

Inconstant Love

Waxing and waning
Like the moon:
Each moon, waxing and waning;
Like one
Never constant
Never harbouring love for long -
O that envy could wane
And love stand true, forever.

Sheila Seecharan